Preface

GW01424275

Based on feedback from some
"*Singapore Maths Model, expla_____ _____ _.___ _ _and 2*"
(*thanks to all who had bought and read it!*), they actually prefer to have more examples on Part-Part-Whole and Comparison Model problems.

Here are **15 Questions** for your child or student to practice. Questions with white space are in the front portion of the book while answers are at the back half of this book. Suggestion is to print the questions (without answers) for the child or student to practice. You can correct and explain with the answers as needed.

As your child or student may need space to draw the models, I will leave each practice question on 1 page, in the view that your child or student has ample space to write and draw the models without cramping 2 or more questions into a single page. These are all sorted at the front of this book for easy printing (if desired).

If you are pressed for time, you can go straight to the answers to get the steps to solve these questions. Practice makes perfect and I hope these questions are useful to ensure your child or student is able to understand and solve these questions if they see them again in future!

Join us at our facebook page to discover future eBooks: https://www.facebook.com/singaporemathsmodel/?ref=bookmarks

Contents

1: The Part-Part-Whole Model Questions

Example PPW-1

Steve has 16 toy cars. Daddy bought him 12 more toy cars. How many toy cars does Steve have altogether?

Example PPW-2

Carmen has 32 dolls. She gave 8 dolls to her best friend.
How many dolls does Carmen have now?

Example PPW-3

Jamie is taking the train to the City. There are 20 stations from where he board to his end destination point. He has travelled past 13 stations. How many more stations must he travel to reach his destination?

Example PPW-4

There are 23 boys and 21 girls in Ian's class. How many pupils are there altogether in Ian's class?

Example PPW-5

Isabella has $18 left after spending $32 on a dress. How much money did she have at first?

2: The Comparison Model Questions

<u>Example CM-1</u>

Ben has 3 toy cars. He has 5 more toy soldiers than toy cars. He has 2 less toy guns then toy soldiers. How many toy guns does Ben have?

Example CM-2

Tim went fishing with his father and grandfather. Tim caught 10 fish. His father caught 8 more fish than Tim. His grandfather caught 3 less fish then his father. How many fish did Tim's grandfather catch?

Example CM-3

Mummy is 37 years old. Daddy is 3 years older than Mummy. Gwen is 30 years younger than Daddy. How old is Gwen?

Example CM-4

Sarah and Natalie have 28 dolls altogether. Sarah has 8 more dolls than Natalie.
    (a) How many dolls does Natalie have?
    (b) How many dolls does Sarah have?

Example CM-5

Bobby is 7 years older than Frank. Their total age is 23 years. How old is Frank?

3: The Combination and Challenging Model Questions

Example COMB-1

There are 13 boys in Tom's class. There are 5 more girls than boys. How many pupils are there altogether in Tom's class?

Example COMB-2

Clarice has 23 stickers. Megan has twice as many stickers as Clarice. How many stickers do they have altogether?

Example COMB-3

Victoria baked 50 cupcakes. She kept 20 cupcakes for her children and gave the rest away to her 2 aunts – Aunt Amy and Aunt Beatrice. Each aunt has the same number of cupcakes. How many cupcakes did Aunt Beatrice have?

Example COMB-4

There are 634 pupils in Grade 1. There are 292 boys in Grade 1. How many more girls are there than boys?

Example COMB-5

There is a rectangular field in school. The length of the rectangle is 66 feet long. The breadth of the rectangle is 26 feet shorter than the length. Ashley ran around the field once. How many feet did Ashley run?

4: Answers to Part-Part-Whole Model Questions

Answers to Example PPW-1

Steve has 16 toy cars. Daddy bought him 12 more toy cars. How many toy cars does Steve have altogether?

Step 1: Draw the 16 toy cars that Steve has now with <u>one</u> rectangle. The object here is "Toy cars".

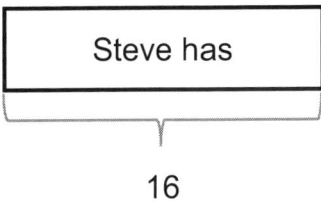

Steve has

16

Step 2: Draw the 12 toy cars that Daddy has bought Steve beside the <u>first</u> rectangle. Since there are 12 toy cars (which is less than 16), this second rectangle should be shorter in length.

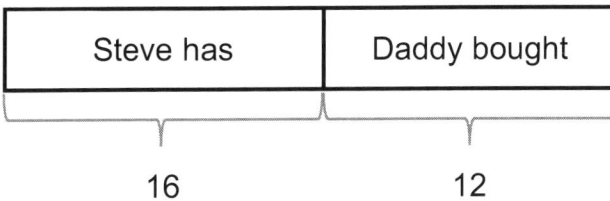

Steve has	Daddy bought

16   12

Step 3: Solve the problem by finding the "?", which is the answer.

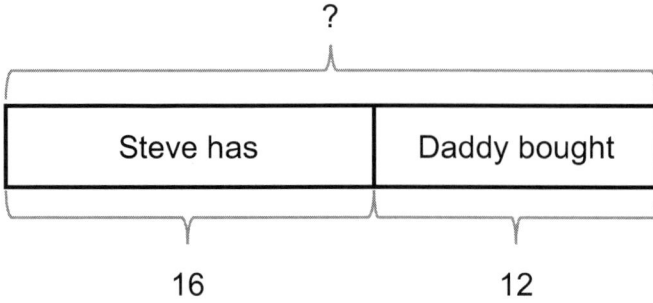

?

Steve has	Daddy bought

16   12

The answer is 16 + 12 = 28.

Steve has 28 toy cars altogether.

Answers to Example PPW-2

Carmen has 32 dolls. She gave 8 dolls to her best friend. How many dolls does Carmen have now?

Step 1: You identify that there is only 1 object – Dolls, therefore you will use the Part-Part-Whole Model.

Draw <u>one</u> rectangle that represents the 32 dolls that Carmen has at the beginning. The object here is "Dolls".

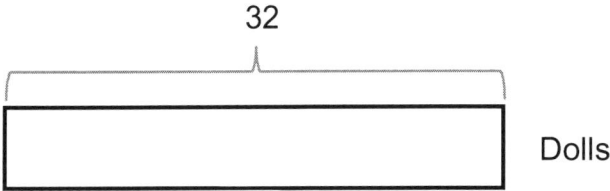

```
              32
    ┌──────────┴──────────┐
    ┌─────────────────────┐
    │                     │  Dolls
    └─────────────────────┘
```

Step 2: Draw a line to split the rectangle into 2 smaller rectangles. Since she gave away 8 dolls, we label this rectangle as "Gave away".

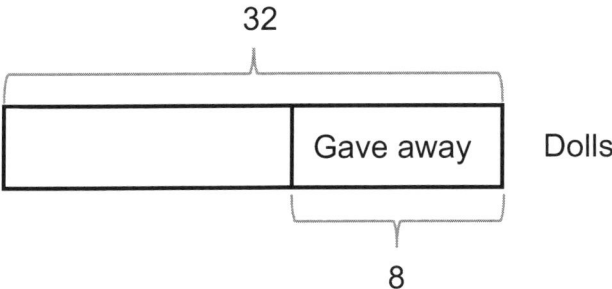

```
              32
    ┌──────────┴──────────┐
    ┌──────────┬──────────┐
    │          │Gave away │  Dolls
    └──────────┴──────────┘
               └────┬────┘
                    8
```

Step 3: We name the other rectangle as "Remaining / Left" representing the number of dolls left. Solve the problem by finding the "?", which is the answer.

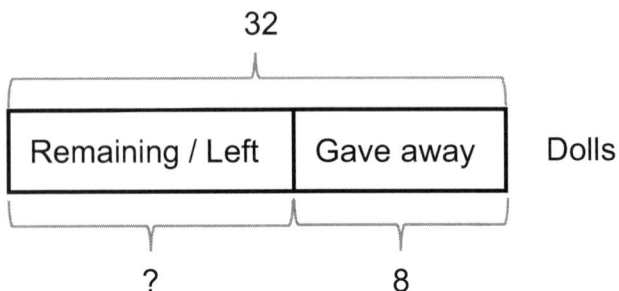

32

Remaining / Left	Gave away	Dolls

? 8

The answer is 32 - 8 = 24.

Carmen has 24 dolls left now.

Answers to Example PPW-3

Jamie is taking the train to the City. There are 20 stations from where he board to his end destination point. He has travelled past 13 stations. How many more stations must he travel to reach his destination?

Step 1: You identify that there is only 1 object – Stations, therefore you will use the Part-Part-Whole Model.

Draw <u>one</u> rectangle that represents the 20 stations that Jamie needs to travel. The object here is "stations".

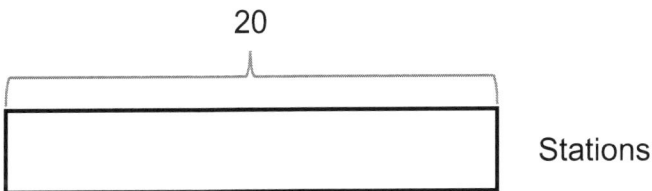

20

Stations

Step 2: Draw a line to split the rectangle into 2 smaller rectangles. Since he has travelled past 13 stations, we label this rectangle as "travelled".

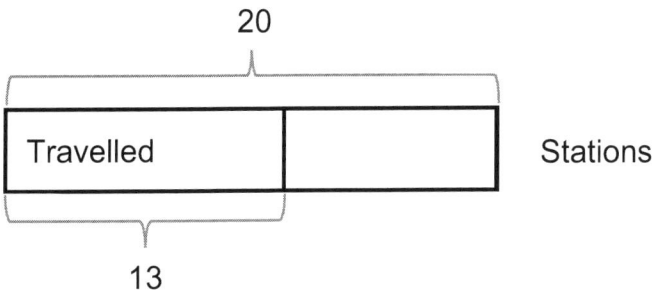

20

Travelled	

Stations

13

Step 3: We name the other rectangle as "Remaining" representing the number of stations left for Jamie to travel. Solve the problem by finding the "?", which is the answer.

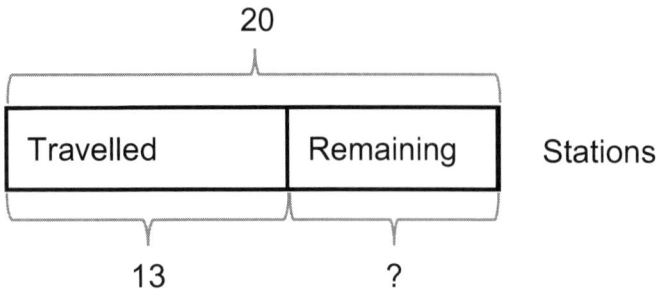

20

| Travelled | Remaining | Stations |

13   ?

The answer is 20 - 13 = 7.

Jamie has to travel 7 more stations before he reach his destination.

<u>Answers to Example PPW-4</u>

There are 23 boys and 21 girls in Ian's class. How many pupils are there altogether in Ian's class?

Step 1: There are boys and girls in a class. All of them are pupils in the class. You identify that there is only 1 object – pupils, therefore you will use the Part-Part-Whole Model.

Draw <u>one</u> rectangle that represents the 23 boys in the class. The object here is "pupils".

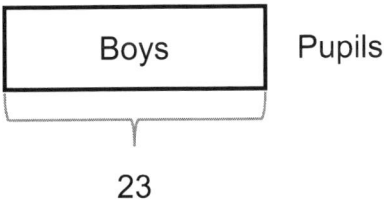

```
┌─────────────────┐
│      Boys       │   Pupils
└─────────────────┘
   _____/
          |
         23
```

Step 2: Draw the 21 girls beside the <u>first</u> rectangle.

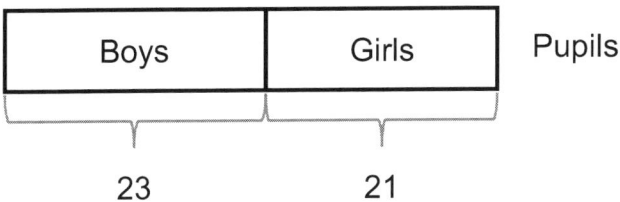

```
┌─────────────┬─────────────┐
│    Boys     │    Girls     │   Pupils
└─────────────┴─────────────┘
  _____/   _____/
       |             |
      23            21
```

Step 3: Solve the problem by finding the "?", which is the answer.

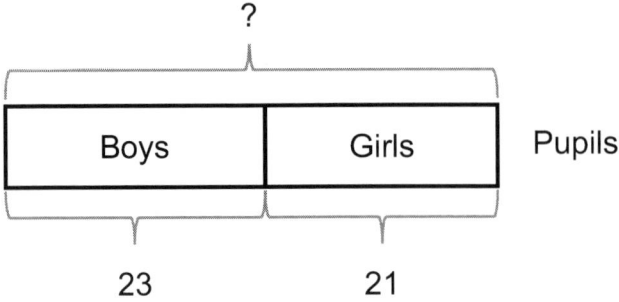

?

Boys	Girls	Pupils

23   21

The answer is 23 + 21 = 44.

There are altogether 44 pupils in Ian's class.

Answers to Example PPW-5

Isabella has $18 left after spending $32 on a dress. How much money did she have at first?

Step 1: Isabella has some money and spent $32 to buy a dress. She has $18 left after buying the dress. You identify that there is only 1 object – money, therefore you will use the Part-Part-Whole Model.

Draw <u>one</u> rectangle that represents the $32 spent on buying a dress. The object here is money using "spent" and "left".

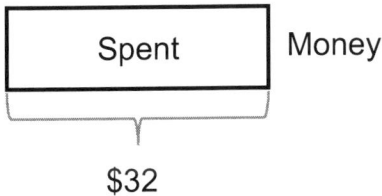

Spent	Money

$32

Step 2: Draw the $18 left beside the <u>first</u> rectangle. Since this is less that the cost of the dress, this rectangle should be shorter in length.

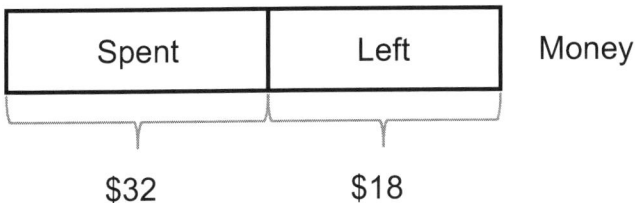

Spent	Left	Money

$32 $18

Step 3: Solve the problem by finding the "?", which is the answer.

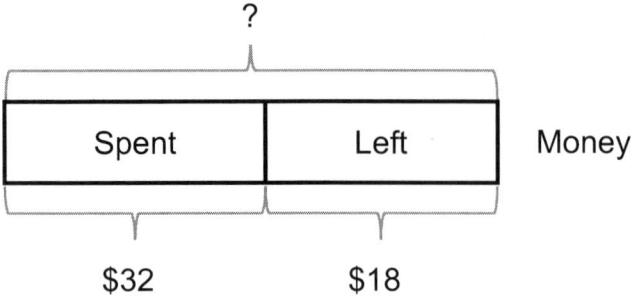

?

Spent	Left

Money

$32 $18

The answer is $32 + $18 = $50.

Isabella had $50 at first.

5: Answers to Comparison Model Questions

Answers to Example CM-1

Ben has 3 toy cars. He has 5 more toy soldiers than toy cars. He has 2 less toy guns then toy soldiers. How many toy guns does Ben have?

Step 1: This is a tricky question as there are 2 parts to solving this question. You will have to find out the number of toy soldiers first, before you can find out the number of toy guns. You identify that there are 3 objects – toy cars, toy soldiers and toy guns, therefore you will use the Comparison Model.

First, you will need to find the number of toy soldiers. Draw the 3 toy cars that Ben has now with <u>one</u> rectangle. The objects here are "toy cars" and "toy soldiers".

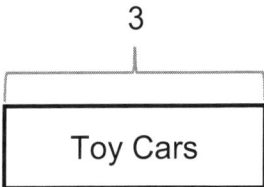

3

Toy Cars

Step 2: Draw a longer rectangle that represents "toy soldiers" *below* the <u>first</u> rectangle. Since we know Ben has 5 *more* toy soldiers than toy cars, this second rectangle should be longer in length.

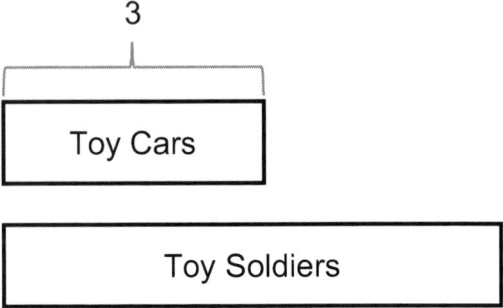

3

Toy Cars

Toy Soldiers

Step 3: Draw the portion where we know there is information. In this case, we know that Ben has 5 more toy soldiers than toy cars. We put the "**5**" beside toy cars' rectangle.

Solve the problem by finding the "?".

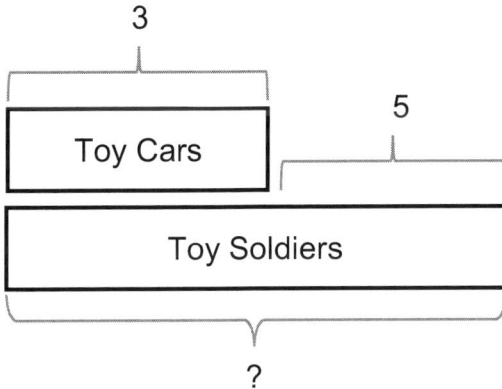

The answer is 3 + 5 = 8. Ben has 8 toy soldiers.

Comments: *We can continue to solve for the number of toy guns, given we now know the number of toy soldiers.*

Step 4: You identify the 2 objects – toy soldiers and toy guns, therefore you continue to use the Comparison Model.

Draw the 8 toy soldiers that Ben has now with <u>one</u> rectangle. The objects here are "toy soldiers" and "toy guns".

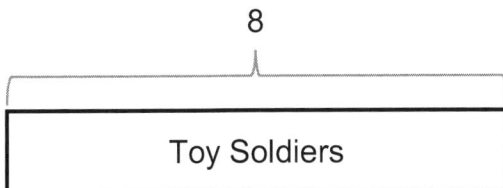

Step 5: Draw a shorter rectangle that represents "toy guns" *below* the <u>first</u> rectangle. Since we know Ben has 2 *less* toy guns than toy soldiers, this second rectangle should be shorter in length.

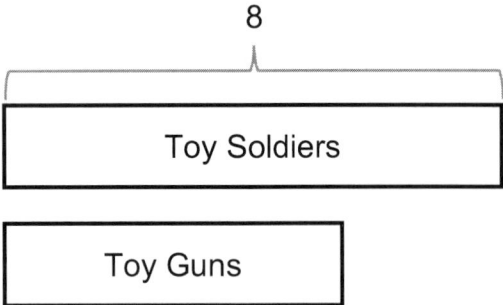

8

```
┌─────────────────────────────┐
│        Toy Soldiers         │
└─────────────────────────────┘

┌─────────────────────┐
│      Toy Guns       │
└─────────────────────┘
```

Step 6: Draw the portion where we know there is information. In this case, we know that Ben has 2 less toy guns than toy soldiers. We put the "*2*" beside toy guns' rectangle.

Solve the problem by finding the "?", which is the answer.

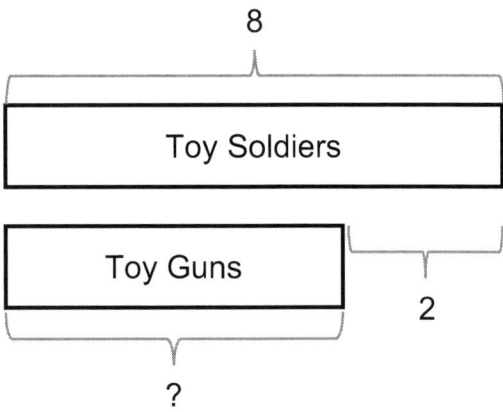

8

```
┌─────────────────────────────┐
│        Toy Soldiers         │
└─────────────────────────────┘

┌─────────────────────┐
│      Toy Guns       │        2
└─────────────────────┘

          ?
```

The answer is 8 - 2 = 6. Ben has 6 toy guns.

Answers to Example CM-2

Tim went fishing with his father and grandfather. Tim caught 10 fish. His father caught 8 more fish than Tim. His grandfather caught 3 less fish then his father. How many fish did Tim's grandfather catch?

Step 1: This is another tricky question as there are 2 parts to solving this question. You will note that although the question is only talking about fish, the object itself is Tim's fish, Tim's father's fish and Tim's grandfather's fish. You identify that there are 3 objects therefore you will use the Comparison Model.

Draw the 10 fish that Tim has caught with <u>one</u> rectangle. The objects here are "Tim's Fish" and "Dad's Fish".

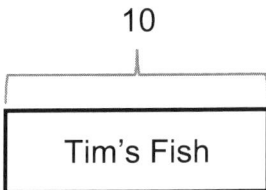

10

Tim's Fish

Step 2: Draw a longer rectangle that represents "Dad's Fish" *below* the <u>first</u> rectangle. Since we know Tim's father has caught 8 *more* fish, this second rectangle should be longer in length.

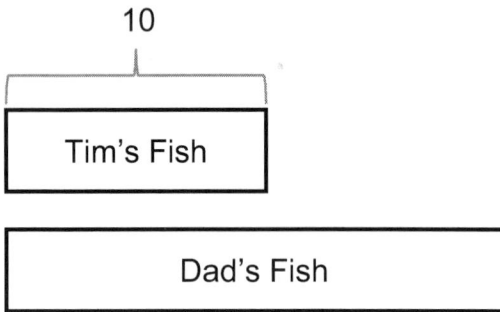

10

Tim's Fish

Dad's Fish

Step 3: Draw the portion where we know there is information. In this case, we know that Tim's father has caught 8 more fish. We put the "*8*" beside "Tim's Fish" rectangle.

Solve the problem by finding the "?".

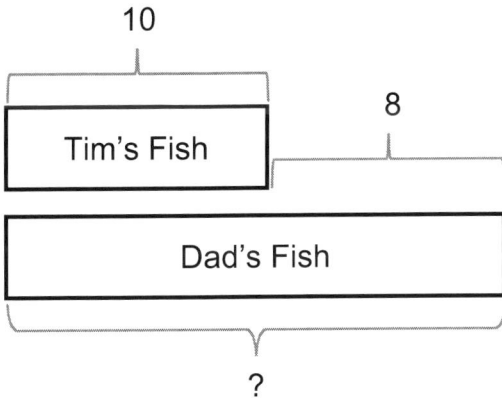

The answer is 10 + 8 = 18.

Tim's father caught 18 fish.

Comments: *We can continue to solve for the number of fish Tim's grandfather caught, given we now know the number of fish Tim's dad has caught.*

Step 4: You identify the 2 objects – Dad's Fish and Grandfather's Fish, therefore you continue to use the Comparison Model.

Draw the 18 fish that Tim's father has caught with <u>one</u> rectangle. The objects here are "Dad's Fish" and "Grandfather's Fish".

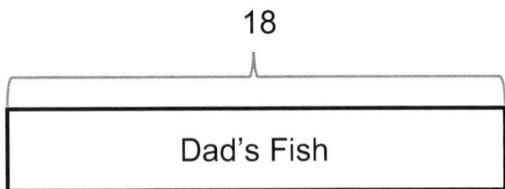

18

Dad's Fish

Step 5: Draw a shorter rectangle that represents "Grandfather's Fish" **below** the <u>first</u> rectangle. Since we know Tim's grandfather has caught 3 **less** fish than Tim's dad, this second rectangle should be shorter in length.

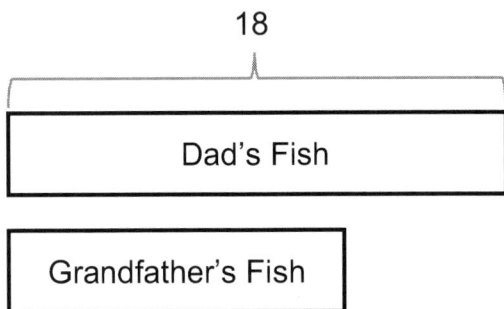

18

Dad's Fish

Grandfather's Fish

Step 6: Draw the portion where we know there is information. In this case, we know that Tim's grandfather has caught 3 less fish than Tim's dad. We put the "**3**" beside "Grandfather's Fish" rectangle.

Solve the problem by finding the "?", which is the answer.

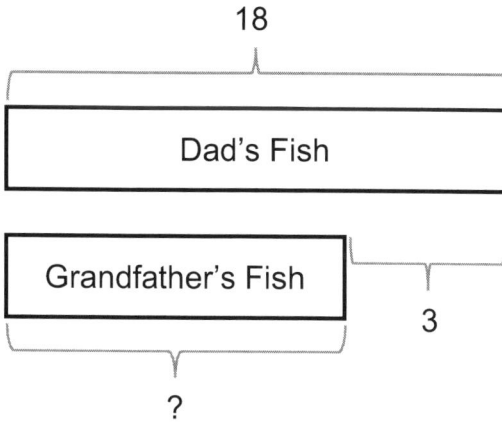

18

Dad's Fish

Grandfather's Fish

3

?

The answer is 18 - 3 = 15.

Tim's grandfather caught 15 fish.

Answers to Example CM-3

Mummy is 37 years old. Daddy is 3 years older than Mummy. Gwen is 30 years younger than Daddy. How old is Gwen?

Step 1: This is another tricky question as there are 2 parts to solving this question. You will note that although the question is only talking about age, the objects are Mummy's age, Daddy's age and Gwen's age. You identify that there are 3 objects therefore you will use the Comparison Model.

Draw Mummy's age with <u>one</u> rectangle. The objects here are "Mummy's Age", "Daddy's Age" and "Gwen's Age".

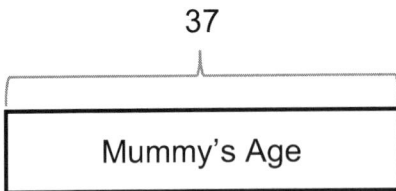

37

Mummy's Age

Step 2: Draw a longer rectangle that represents "Daddy's Age" *below* the <u>first</u> rectangle. Since we know Daddy is 3 years *older* than Mummy, this second rectangle should be longer in length.

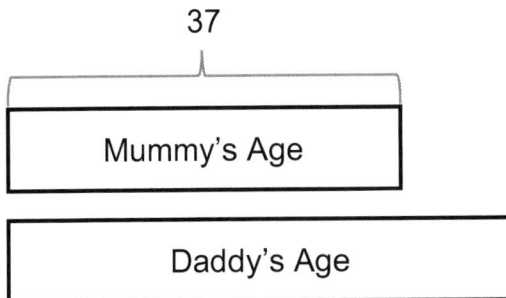

37

Mummy's Age

Daddy's Age

Step 3: Draw the portion where we know there is information. In this case, we know that Daddy is 3 years older than Mummy. We put the "**3**" beside "Mummy's Age" rectangle.

Solve the problem by finding the "?".

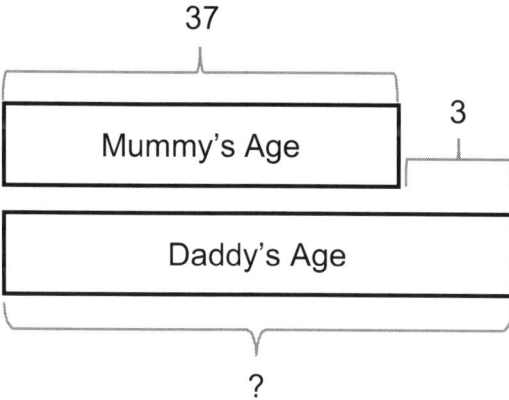

37

Mummy's Age

3

Daddy's Age

?

The answer is 37 + 3 = 40.

Daddy is 40 years old.

Comments: *We can continue to solve for Gwen's age by comparing her age with Daddy. Here, we will add the comparison rectangle to the existing Model.*

Step 4: You continue to use the Comparison Model, adding Gwen's age at the bottom.

Draw a rectangle representing "Gwen's Age" below "Daddy's Age". This should be much shorter in length as we know Gwen is 30 years younger than Daddy. We redraw "Daddy's Age" of "40" at the side (instead of bottom).

Comments: The "Gwen's Age" rectangle need not be in exact proportion to "Mummy's Age" and "Daddy's Age" rectangles. We just need to draw "Gwen's Age" much shorter than the other 2 rectangles to understand Gwen is much younger than her parents.

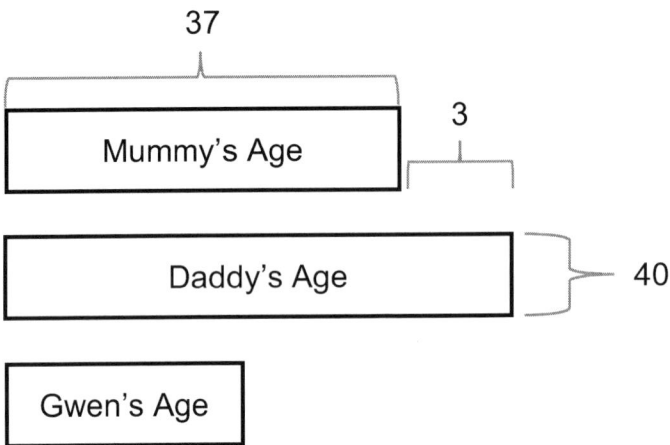

37

Mummy's Age

3

Daddy's Age   40

Gwen's Age

Step 5: Draw the portion where we know there is information. In this case, we know that Gwen is 30 years younger than Daddy. We put the "*30*" beside "Gwen's Age" rectangle.

Solve the problem by finding the "?", which is the answer.

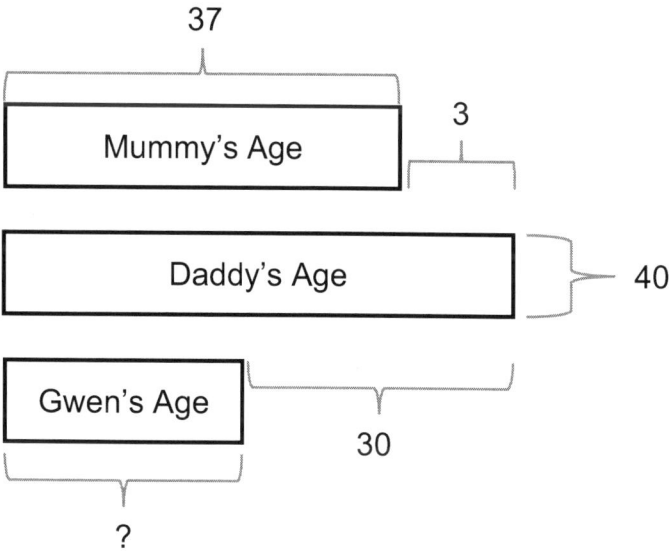

The answer is 40 - 30 = 10.

Gwen is 10 years old.

Sarah and Natalie have 28 dolls altogether. Sarah has 8 more dolls than Natalie.

(a) How many dolls does Natalie have?

(b) How many dolls does Sarah have?

Step 1: There are 2 parts to solving this question. You will note that we have to solve for how many dolls both Natalie and Sarah each has. Although the question is only talking about dolls, we are actually comparing how many dolls Sarah and Natalie have. You identify that "Sarah's Dolls" and "Natalie's Dolls" are 2 objects, you will adopt the Comparison Model.

First we know Sarah has more dolls than Natalie. Draw one rectangle to represent Sarah's Dolls. The objects here are "Sarah's Dolls" and "Natalie's Dolls".

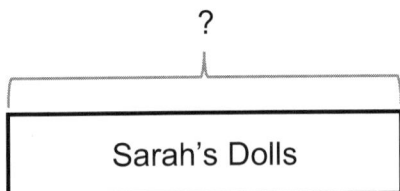

?

Sarah's Dolls

42

Step 2: Draw a shorter rectangle that represents "Natalie's Dolls" **below** the first rectangle. Since we know Sarah has 8 **more** dolls than Natalie, this second rectangle should be shorter in length.

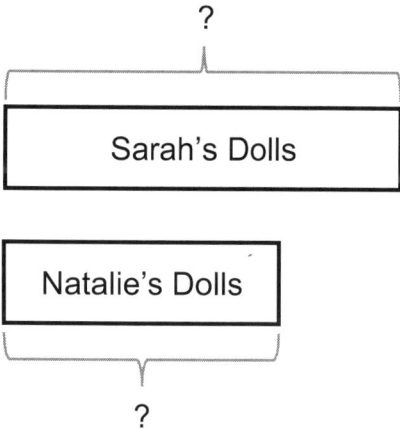

?

Sarah's Dolls

Natalie's Dolls

?

Step 3: Draw the portion where we know there is information. In this case, we know that Sarah has 8 more dolls than Natalie. We put the "8 more" beside Natalie's rectangle. We also know, Sarah and Natalie have 28 dolls altogether. We can put the total number of dolls at the side.

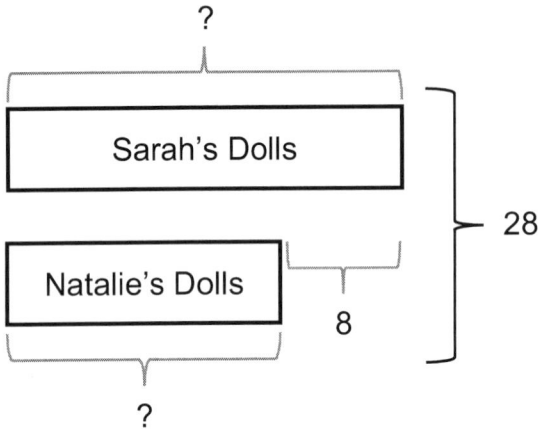

Comments: You will note that by subtracting the total of 28 dolls against the "8 more" dolls that Sarah has, does not give you the answer of how many dolls either Sarah or Natalie has.

We need to draw an additional dotted line to see that the remaining number of dolls are equal. This equal portion of the remaining dolls is what Natalie has.

Step 4: You draw a dotted line from the end of Natalie's rectangle into Sarah's rectangle. Visually, the 2 rectangles are of the same size. Therefore the sum of these 2 equal-sized rectangles is the difference between the total (28) and what Sarah has more over Natalie (8).

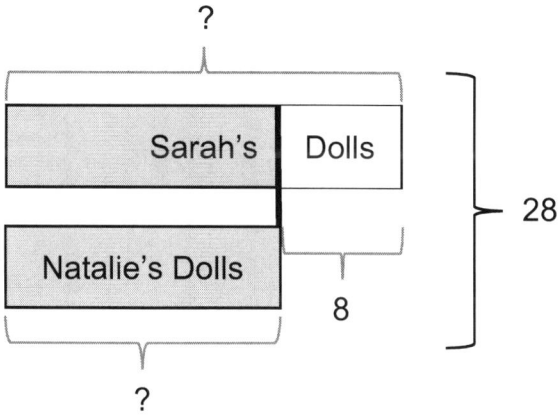

?

Sarah's | Dolls

28

Natalie's Dolls

8

?

The 2 Yellow shaded rectangles (equal-sized) = 28 – 8 = 20

Which leads us to: 10 + 10 = 20

(A) Therefore Natalie has 10 dolls (which is equal to 1 Yellow shaded rectangle).

Step 5: We know Sarah has 8 more dolls than Natalie. In step 4, we have already solved that Natalie has 10 dolls.

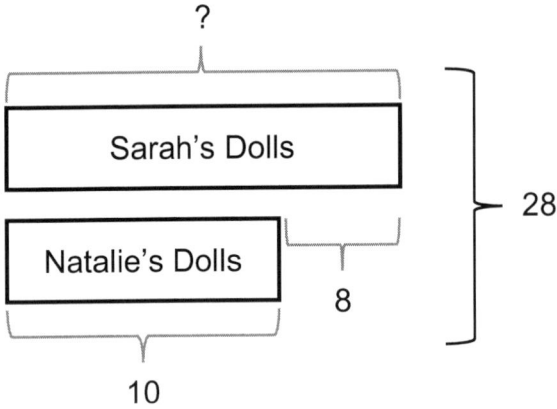

Which leads us to: 10 + 8 = 18

(B) Therefore Sarah has 18 dolls.

Answers to Example CM-5

Bobby is 7 years older than Frank. Their total age is 23 years. How old is Bobby?

Step 1: There are 2 parts to solving this question. You will note that we have to solve for how Frank and Bobby is. Although the question is only talking about age, we are actually comparing how old Bobby is against Frank. You identify that "Bobby's Age" and "Frank's Age" are 2 objects, you will adopt the Comparison Model.

First we know Bobby is older than Frank. Draw <u>one</u> rectangle to represent "Bobby's Age". The objects here are "Bobby's Age" and "Frank's Age".

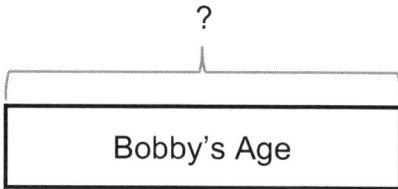

?

Bobby's Age

Step 2: Draw a shorter rectangle that represents "Frank's Age" *below* the <u>first</u> rectangle. Since we know Bobby is *older* than Frank, this second rectangle should be shorter in length.

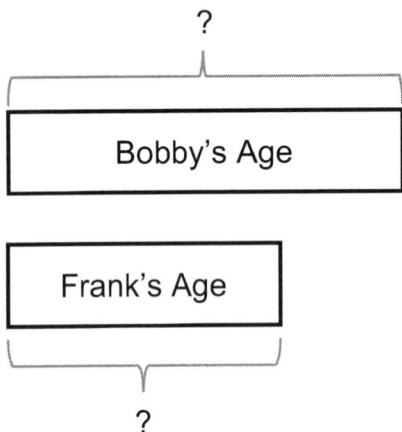

?

Bobby's Age

Frank's Age

?

Step 3: Draw the portion where we know there is information. In this case, we know that Bobby is 7 years older than Frank. We put the "7" beside Frank's rectangle. We also know, Bobby and Frank are 23 years altogether. We can put the total age at the side.

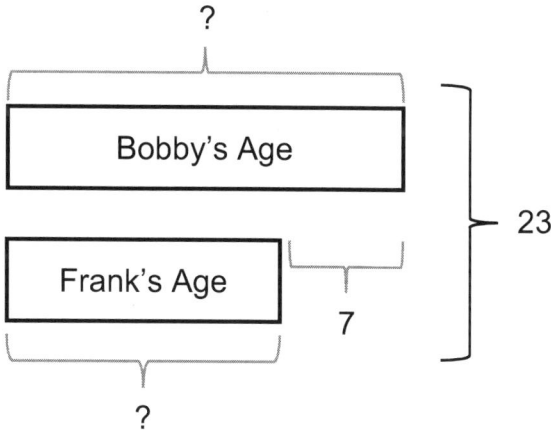

Comments: You will note that you the answer of how old either Bobby or Frank is.

We need to draw an additional dotted line to see that the remaining "years" are equal. This equal portion is Frank's age.

Step 4: You draw a dotted line from the end of Frank's rectangle into Bobby's rectangle. Visually, the 2 rectangles are of the same size. Therefore the sum of these 2 equal-sized rectangles is the difference between the total age (23) and how many years Bobby is older than Frank (7).

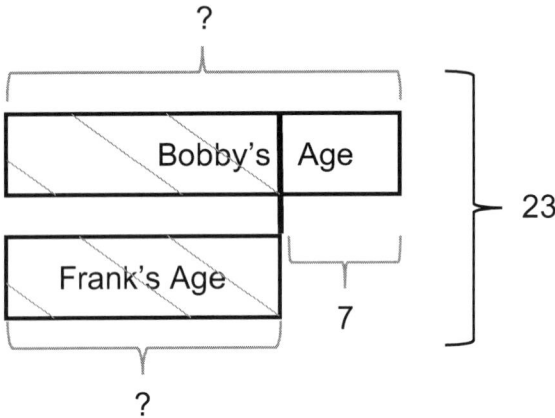

The 2 diagonally-shaded rectangles (equal-sized)
= 23 – 7
= 16

Which leads us to: 8 + 8 = 16

Therefore Frank is 8 years old (which is equal to 1 diagonally-shaded rectangle).

Step 5: We know Bobby is 7 years older than Frank. In step 4, we have already solved that Frank is 8 years old.

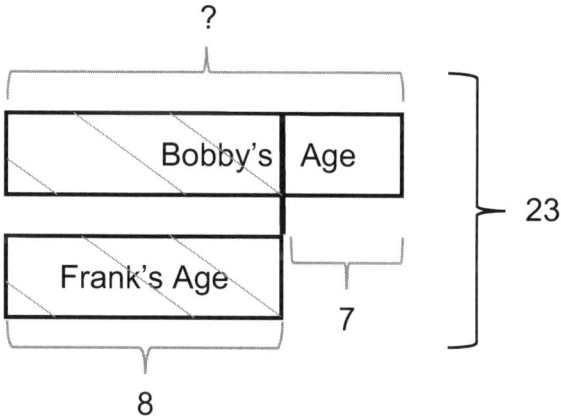

Which leads us to: 8 + 7 = 15

Therefore Bobby is 15 years old.

6: Answers to Combination and Challenging Model Questions

Answers to Example COMB-1

There are 13 boys in Tom's class. There are 5 more girls than boys. How many pupils are there altogether in Tom's class?

Step 1: There are 2 parts to solving this question. You will note that we have to solve for how girls there are in the class first. You identify that "Boys" and "Girls" are 2 objects, you will adopt the Comparison Model.

Draw <u>one</u> rectangle to represent "Boys". The objects here are "Boys" and "Girls".

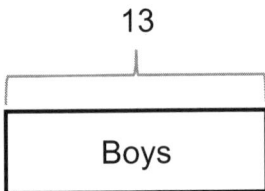

13

Boys

Step 2: Draw a longer rectangle that represents "Girls" **below** the first rectangle. Since we know there are 5 **more** girls than boys, this second rectangle should be longer in length.

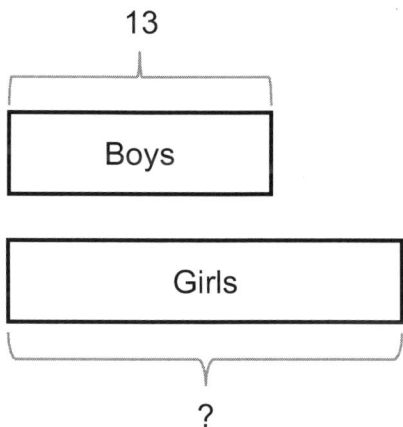

13

| Boys |

| Girls |

?

Step 3: Draw the portion where we know there is information. In this case, we know that there are 5 more girls than boys. We put the "**5**" beside "Boys" rectangle.

Solve the problem by finding the "?".

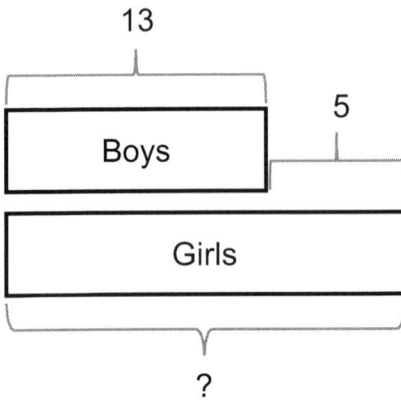

13

| Boys |
| Girls |

5

?

The answer is 13 + 5 = 18.

There are 18 girls in Tim's class.

Step 4: You need to solve how many pupils there are in Tim's class. Here you will note that boys and girls are both pupils in Tim's class, therefore there is 1 object. You will use the Part-Part-Whole Model. As you have already solved for the number of girls, you can put the information together to solve for the total number of pupils. Since there are more girls than boys, the "Girls" rectangle will be longer than the "Boys" rectangle.

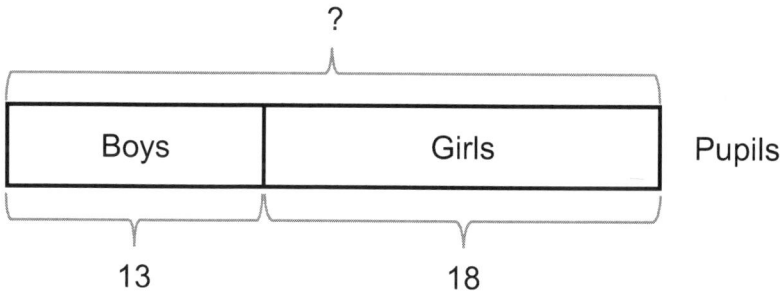

?

| Boys | Girls | Pupils |

13   18

The answer is 13 + 18 = 31.

There are 31 pupils in Tom's Class.

Answers to Example COMB-2

Clarice has 23 stickers. Megan has twice as many stickers as Clarice. How many stickers do they have altogether?

Step 1: There are 2 parts to solving this question. You will note that we have to solve how many stickers does Megan has. You identify that "Clarice's Stickers" and "Megan's Stickers" are 2 objects, you will adopt the Comparison Model.

Draw <u>one</u> rectangle to represent "Clarice's Stickers". The objects here are "Clarice's Stickers" and "Megan's Stickers".

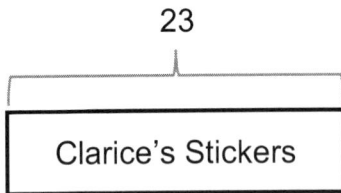

23

Clarice's Stickers

Step 2: Draw a longer rectangle that represents "Megan's Stickers" *below* the <u>first</u> rectangle. Since we know there are Megan has *twice* as many stickers, this second rectangle should be longer in length.

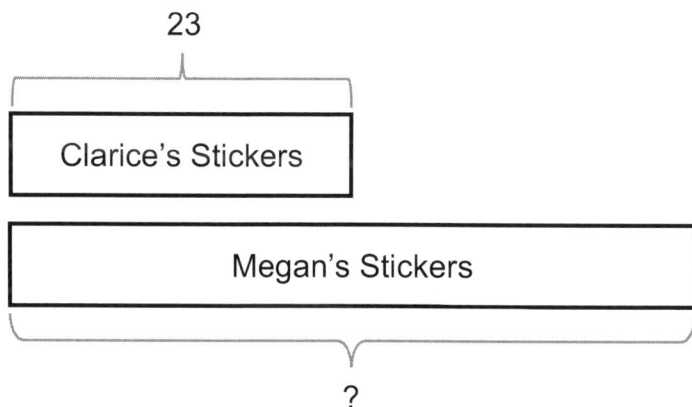

23

Clarice's Stickers

Megan's Stickers

?

Step 3: Draw the portion where we know there is information. In this case, we know that Megan has **twice** as many stickers as Clarice. This means Megan has exactly **23 more** stickers than Clarice. We put the "**23**" beside "Clarice's Stickers" rectangle.

Solve the problem by finding the "?".

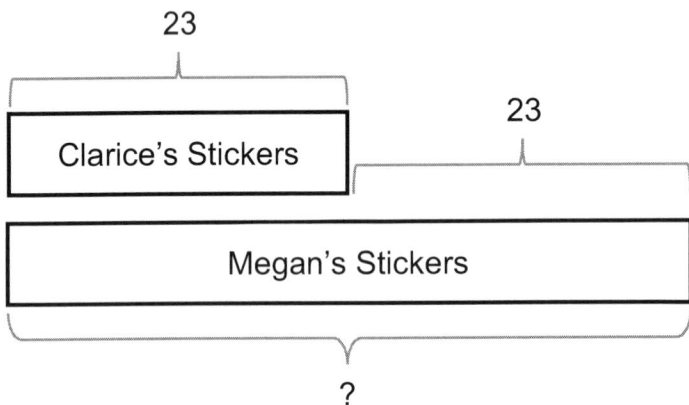

The answer is 23 + 23 = 46.

Megan has 46 stickers.

Step 4: You need to solve how many stickers both Clarice and Megan have altogether. Since there is only 1 object – Stickers, you will use the Part-Part-Whole Model. As you have already solved for the number stickers Megan has, you can put the information together to solve for the total number of stickers. Since Megan has twice as many stickers as Clarice, the "Megan's Stickers" rectangle will be longer than the "Clarice's Stickers" rectangle.

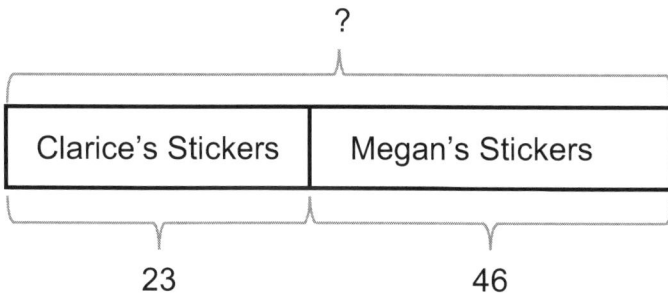

```
                              ?

   ┌──────────────────┬────────────────────┐
   │ Clarice's Stickers │  Megan's Stickers  │
   └──────────────────┴────────────────────┘
          23                    46
```

The answer is 23 + 46 = 69.

Clarice and Megan have 69 stickers altogether.

Comments: You may ask, can we just sum up using the Comparison Model and not use Part-Part-Whole to get the total number of stickers? Yes you CAN! The diagram below shows how and the equation is the same. However, some children will find using the Part-Part-Whole Model gives them more clarity in getting the total answer.

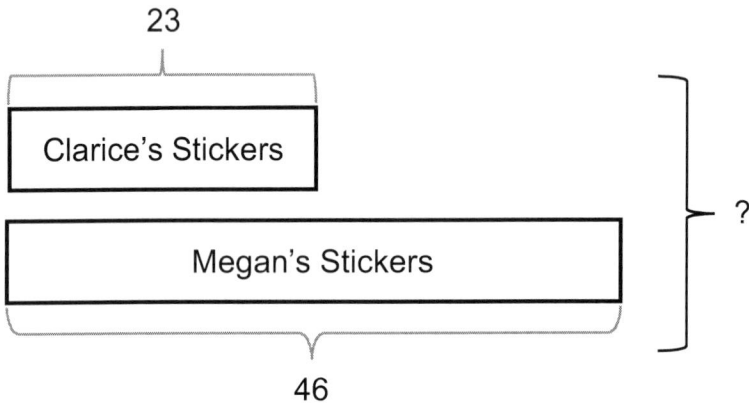

23

| Clarice's Stickers |
| Megan's Stickers |

?

46

Answers to Example COMB-3

Victoria baked 50 cupcakes. She kept 20 cupcakes for her children and gave the rest away to her 2 aunts – Aunt Amy and Aunt Beatrice. Each aunt has the same number of cupcakes. How many cupcakes did Aunt Beatrice have?

Step 1: There are 2 parts to solving this question. First, you will solve how many cupcakes were given to the 2 aunts. You identify that there is 1 object "Cupcakes" and you will adopt the Part-Part-Whole Model.

Draw <u>one</u> rectangle to represent the number of cupcakes "Kept". The objects here are "Kept" and "Gave Away".

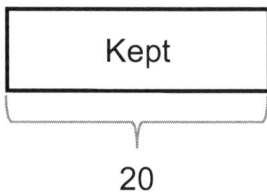

Step 2: Draw a longer rectangle that represents "Gave Away" ***beside*** the <u>first</u> rectangle. Since we know there are 20 left (less than half of 50), this second rectangle should be longer in length.

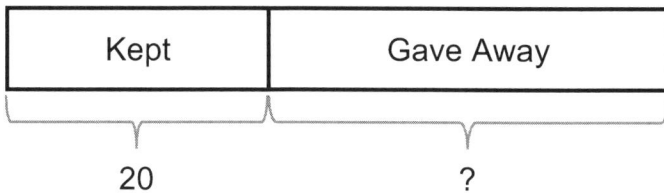

Step 3: Draw the portion where we know there is information. In this case, we know that Victoria baked 50 cupcakes. We put the "**50**" on top of the two rectangles.

Solve the problem by finding the "?".

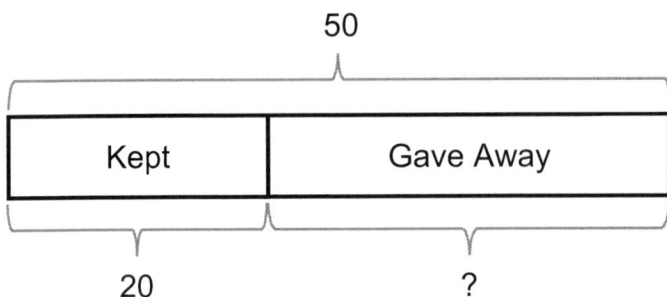

50

Kept	Gave Away

20   ?

The answer is 50 – 20 = 30.

Victoria gave away 30 cupcakes to Aunt Amy and Aunt Beatrice.

Step 4: You note that Aunt Amy and Aunt Beatrice have 30 cupcakes altogether. We know that both Aunt Amy and Aunt Beatrice have the same number of cupcakes. Since we are comparing Aunt Amy's cupcakes against Aunt Beatrice's cupcakes, we will use the Comparison Model. The objects are "Aunt Amy" and "Aunt Beatrice". Since they have the same number of cupcakes, their rectangles are similar in size.

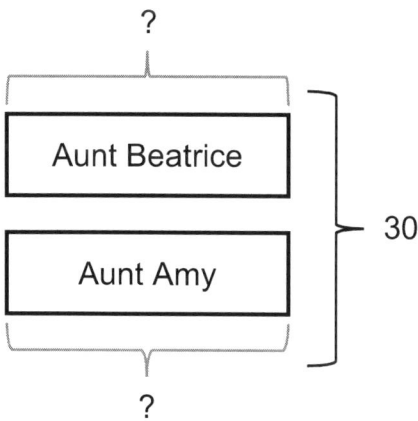

?

Aunt Beatrice

30

Aunt Amy

?

The answer is 15 + 15 = 30.

Aunt Beatrice has 15 cupcakes.

Answers to Example COMB-4

There are 634 pupils in Grade 1. There are 292 boys in Grade 1. How many more girls are there than boys?

Step 1: There are 2 parts to solving this question. First, you will solve how many girls there are in Grade 1. You identify that there is 1 object "Pupils" and you will adopt the Part-Part-Whole Model.

Draw <u>one</u> rectangle to represent the number of "Boys". The objects here are "Boys" and "Girls", which both are pupils of Grade 1.

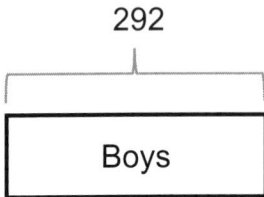

292

```
┌─────────────┐
│             │
│    Boys     │
│             │
└─────────────┘
```

Step 2: Draw a longer rectangle that represents "Girls" *beside* the <u>first</u> rectangle. Since we know there are more girls than boys, this second rectangle should be longer in length.

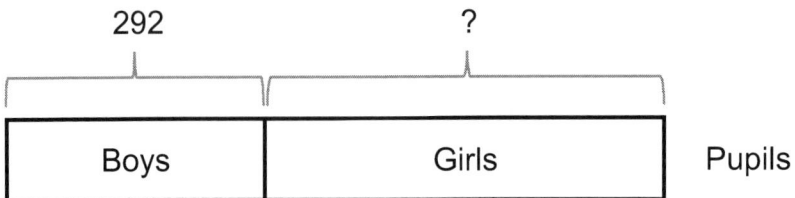

292   ?

```
┌──────────┬────────────────┐
│          │                │
│   Boys   │     Girls      │   Pupils
│          │                │
└──────────┴────────────────┘
```

Step 3: Draw the portion where we know there is information. In this case, we know that there are 634 pupils in Grade. We put the "**634**" at the bottom of the two rectangles.

Solve the problem by finding the "?".

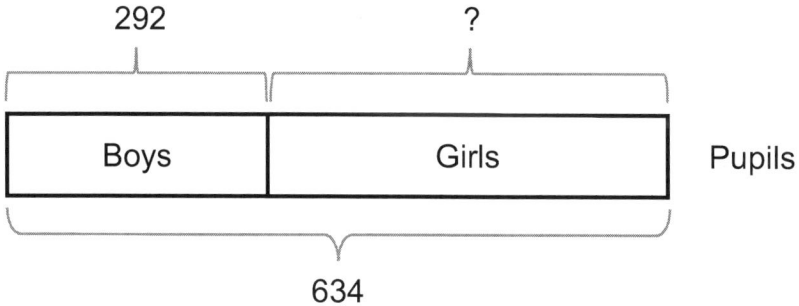

The answer is 634 − 292 = 342.

There are 342 girls in Grade 1.

Step 4: We know there are 342 girls in Grade 1. Since we are comparing Girls against Boys, we will use the Comparison Model. The objects are "Boys" and "Girls". Draw a rectangle to represent Boys.

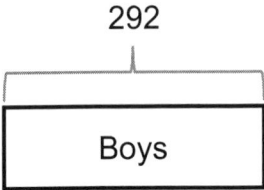

292

Boys

Step 5: Draw a longer rectangle that represents "Girls" **below** the first rectangle. Since we know there are **more** girls than boys, this second rectangle should be longer in length.

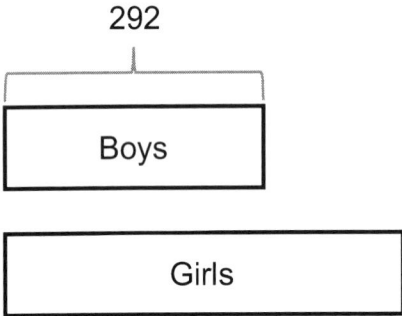

292

Boys

Girls

Step 6: Draw the portion where we know there is information. In this case, we know that there are 342 girls. We put the "**?**" beside "Boys" rectangle.

Solve the problem by finding the "?".

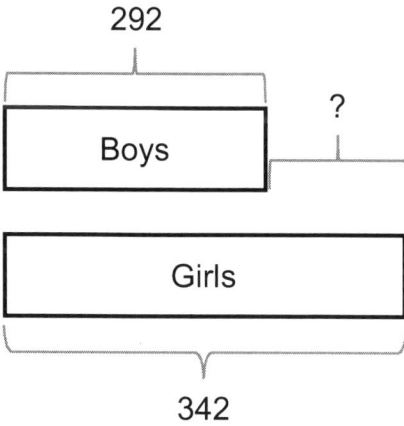

292

Boys

?

Girls

342

The answer is 342 – 292 = 50.

There are 50 more girls than boys in Grade 1.

Answers to Example COMB-5

There is a rectangular field in school. The length of the rectangle is 66 feet long. The breadth of the rectangle is 26 feet shorter than the length. Ashley ran around the field once. How many feet did Ashley run?

Step 1: There are 2 parts to solving this question. First you can draw a rectangle to represent the field.

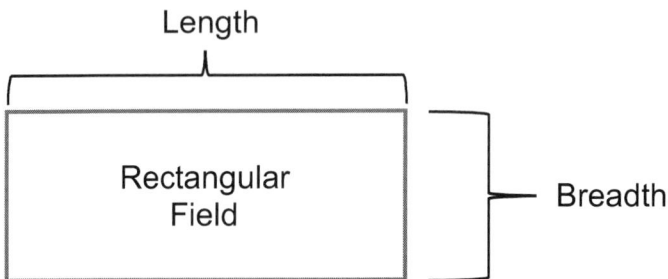

Length

Rectangular
Field

Breadth

Next, you will solve how long the breadth of the rectangular field. You identify that there are 2 objects "Length" and "Breadth", therefore you will adopt the Comparison Model.

Draw <u>one</u> rectangle to represent the "Length". The objects here are "Length" and "Breadth".

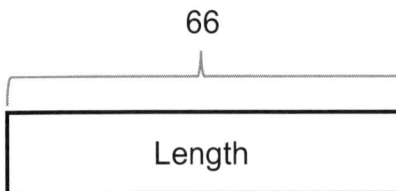

66

Length

Step 2: Draw a shorter rectangle that represents "Breadth" *below* the <u>first</u> rectangle. Since we know the "Breadth" is shorter by 26 feet, this second rectangle should be shorter in length.

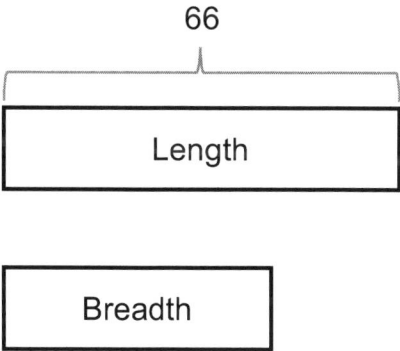

66

Length

Breadth

Step 3: Draw the portion where we know there is information. In this case, we know that the "Breadth" is shorter that the "Length" by 26 feet. We put the "**26**" beside the "Breadth" rectangle.

Solve the problem by finding the "?".

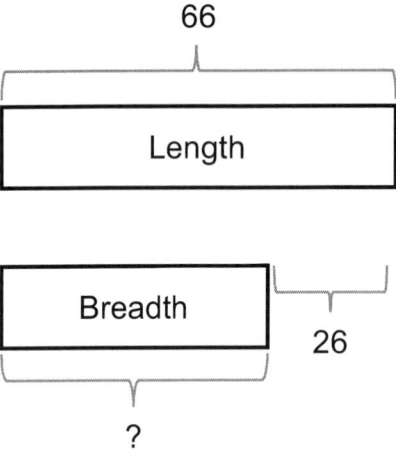

66

Length

Breadth

26

?

The answer is 66 – 26 = 40.

The Breadth of the rectangular field is 40 feet long.

Step 4: Ashley ran round the rectangular field once. You identify that there is 1 object "Feet" and use the Part-Part-Whole Model. To find the total distance that Ashley ran, we have to add all the parts that Ashley ran.

We can now draw all the rectangles that represent the Length and Breadth that Ashley ran into 1 diagram.

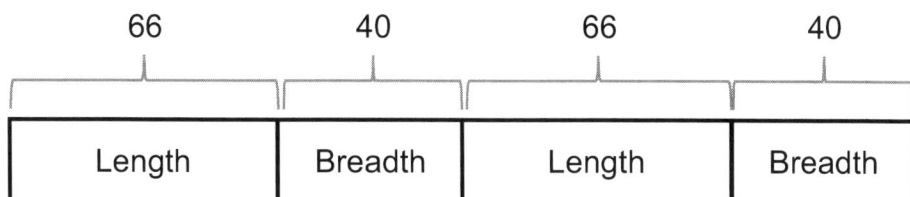

66	40	66	40
Length	Breadth	Length	Breadth

The answer is 66 + 40 + 66 + 40 = 212.

Ashley ran 212 feet by running around the rectangular field once.

31811455R00039

Printed in Great Britain
by Amazon